FIDELEM EXPECTATIONEM

FIDELEM EXPECTATIONEM

POETIC REFLECTIONS FOR ADVENT AND OTHER SPECIAL OCCASIONS

VICTOR A. DIRKS

with
WESLEY A. THIESSEN

Fidelem Expectationum: Poetic Reflections for Advent and Other Special Occasions.

Copyright © 2021 by Wesley A Thiessen. All rights reserved. These poems were the work of Victor A. Dirks, now deceased, but remain the property of his family, and his friends, those to whom these poems were given.

ISBN
978-1-7776615-6-4 (paperback)
978-1-7776615-7-1 (ebook)

Cover design concept: Elaine Thiessen
Cover font: Wonderful Branding

Printed on demand. No part of this book may be used or reproduced in any manner whatsoever without the written permission except in the case of brief quotations embodied in critical articles and reviews, or the copying of a single poem for personal or non-commercial use.

For book information, address:
MOF Publishing, RR 1, Blackie, AB T0L 0J0 Canada.
Email: mofpublishing@proinbox.com
MOF Publishing website: http://www.mofpublishing.com

For my Family

CONTENTS

Acknowledgments ix
Foreword xi

Christmas Poems 1
Christmas Greetings 1972-1995 3
Mystery 5
Christmas in Canada 7
Advent Reflections 9
Settled at Christmas 11
Christmas Morning 13
Christmas Eve 15
Christmas Snow 17
Thoughts 19
December Evening 21
Christmas Joy 23
In Time of Change 25
Through Christmas into a New year 27
Lights Coming On 29
Thoughts in Season 31
Reflections on Christmas 33
Homelessness 35
Of Time and Christmas 37
In Convertendo 39
Sweet Fragile Sounds 41
Be Not Afraid 43
Hard Times and Christmases 45
Let Hope Return 47
And Still Comes 49
Christmas Poems 1996-2010 51
Return To Joy 53
Reborn 55
Contrasts 57
Not Alone 59
Reflections 61
Healing 63
Celebration 65
Advent Prayer 67
Again It's Christmas 69
Advent Prayer 71

Touch of a Hand	73
Christmas Thoughts	75
Tidings In Troubled Times	77
Christmas Restores	79
A Dream of Christmas Day	81
Family Photos	83
Untitled	85
Easter Sonnets	89
Good Friday 1975	91
Holy Saturday 1975	93
Easter 1975	95
Easter in Ontario, 1978	97
Easter 1982	99
Wedding Poems	101
White Oak Road Bride	103
To Carol	105
Wedding Thoughts	107
Gina	109
Special Occasion Poems	111
God Uses who He Chooses	113
The Lord of History	115
Uncertain Times with Certainty	117
Birthday Celebrations	119
Hubert	121
Trust	125
A House Remains	127
Homecoming	129
Advent 2004 (Prose)	131
Witness	133
Birthday Salute	135
One Hundred Years	137
Presence	139
Advent and Always	141
Blessed Departure	143
A Century	145
St. Paul's Cathedral	147
Morning	155
Mourning	157
For Neil	159

ACKNOWLEDGMENTS

Thanks to my mother, Rosemarie Thiessen, who collected preserved and gave impetus for this project. Thanks also to my Aunt Marguerite Dyke for providing a missing advent poem. Thanks to my Aunt Elisabeth for providing the family photos and those of the house at 210 Cheriton Avenue in Winnipeg. Thanks to Norman Barton for providing the photo of Victor and Margaret. Thanks to God also, for the lives we have lived which have made this collection possible.

FOREWORD

I recall a visit Uncle Victor made to our home in Calgary, AB, along with his first wife, Frances, when I was still a young boy. While many adults would have noted that he created conflict with his strong opinions, I was intrigued by my mother's oldest brother who left a robust impression on me, even then. Like a heavy-weight boxer, he entered the "ring" of almost every conversation fully alert to his opponent. His verbal expertise made him a formidable sparring partner and kept him in the limelight of conversation. He was what we called, "larger than life."

He maintained these family connections through long missives, again displaying his literary skills. The easily identifiable letters from him arrived in our mailbox more frequently than from almost anyone else. With distinctively slanted cursive handwriting flowing like a river on the page, he made even the most simple of written tasks, an envelope, look elegant

As a new graduate student traveling overseas I arranged to leave my vehicle parked in his garage in Ontario, just over 3,000 km from my home. On my departure overseas, I wasn't aware that my uncle's political opinions of the Middle East would evoke such strong responses from me—I was headed to Jerusalem. During my two years in Jerusalem I received some of those beautifully hand-addressed envelopes, as Uncle Victor began to write to me, his nephew, studying in the Holy Land. We developed a friendship through that correspondence, touching on topics both personal and public. I learned how widely read and educated Uncle Victor was, and how boldly he would declare his opinions—a challenge for the mediator heart in me. Once I understood more about Uncle Victor and his seemingly eccentric life, I began to take a greater interest in his writing, soon after realizing his gifted ability to write poetry. His Advent poems became an annual focus.

Not much later, I had occasion to commission a poem by my uncle, expressing my desire that he should write a poem to celebrate the occasion of my marriage. I have never been able to discern the reason for the delay, the wedding having taken place in September, with the poem arriving the following May. Nonetheless, he solidified the act through the use of pen and paper, honouring me and my wife Elaine, through his poetic script.

Uncle Victor continued to write and follow my life's journey, however my choice to move to the Arab world in 1997 seemed to put our relationship on hold. His Zionist leanings challenged his understanding of how an educated family member of his would intentionally spend years of their life living in the Muslim world. We lacked the luxury of lengthy personal visits together to fully discuss this subject, leaving me confident there were things left unsaid he would have wanted me to know.

As many sages have observed, we rarely recognize the true value of some things until we have them no longer. My friendship with Uncle Victor allowed me to see my extended family and their legacy in my life from a different perspective. His input enriched my life with a window in to the lives of my grandparents, who had both passed away prior to my travels overseas. By knowing Victor, I came to better understand my forefathers and their journey from the "old country." The place and person I am today, and the potential for so much of what I've done and still can do is in large part a reflection of the spiritual background of my parents, grandparents and those before them. These generations have deposited values of honesty, integrity, hard work, justice and faith in God into our spiritual DNA, providing for me and many of my relatives the firm foundation upon which to build a stable life. We reap benefits because of the sacrifices of our ancestors. This may be a widespread or even universal experience. I'm sure I'm not the only one who has had this experience. The poems, and primarily the ones written for Advent, are a literary example of the legacy of faith which I believe has been passed down to me through the faith of my forefathers and foremothers.

It was a treat to look forward to Uncle Victor's advent poem each year, something I have missed over the past decade and some. For a few years now I have wanted to gather his poems together in a more permanent fashion. The idea was originally my mother's and we initially collaborated on the project. After it was set aside a few times, I picked it up recently, spurred on by family events and another fast approaching Advent. Knowing that life is uncertain I am anxious to complete the project while other family members can enjoy it. I am delighted that I can now finally pass this collection of poems on to others to share in the experience of reflecting on Advent and other seasons of faith. In this collected form, I also share my own legacy of hope, light, and love.

Uncle Victor liked to use Latin from time to time in his poetry. With this in mind, I have crafted a title in Latin, *Fidelem Expectationum*. *Fidelem* means faith and many may recall the Latin carol *Adeste Fidelus*, translated *O Come All Ye Faithful*. *Expectationum* brings with it the meaning of waiting, like the entire season of Advent, when we await the One who reconciles us with the great I Am. The idea here is of expectant faith, or faith that waits patiently, yet fully alive with hope. Advent does this for me every year, as I'm sure it does for many others. Maybe this season also brings you back to similar reflections on those who went before you and laid spiritual foundations for you. Advent is a time that connects us—to each other, to our past, to our faith.

May these poems help you to reflect on what God has done for us, and bring you closer to the knowledge of his great love for you—coming in flesh, God with us, Emmanuel.

CHRISTMAS POEMS

CHRISTMAS GREETINGS 1972-1995

MYSTERY
FIRST READ BY MARY ANN RATZLAFF, MINNEAPOLIS

What was
Is now
Because
Somehow
God came!

Through birth
By maid
Our earth
To aid.
Reclaim.

To beast
And bird
The feast
Deferred
Proclaim.

For man
From sin
Now can
Come in
To Peace.

CHRISTMAS IN CANADA
ON VICTORIA AVE., NEAR VINELAND

From peach to pine to farthest north
From sea to sea, a light shines forth
Mid winter snow.

O glorious mystery sublime
Anew revealed in northern clime:
The Rose aglow!

Our reason, value, sense of place
And order, crashes on its face:
A baby cries

Our wisdom is at naught, undone
For with that birthwail has begun
A claim of prize.

And so we come, bowed down and pressed
By every guilt, with chains oppressed.
And are made free.

What other mark of kingship is?
Redemptor, Liberator? This
Is David's tree.

Your infant needs are food, warmth, rest...
You take them from your mother's breast
As offering.

Here rebel and republican
Must join us monarchists who can
Accept a king.

Here can no mighty men avail
The gates of Hell shall not prevail
Against you, Word.

Be Wonderful, be Counsellor
Our Prince of Peace ... and lo, therefore
Our mighty Lord

ADVENT REFLECTIONS
IN KINGSVILLE

A year ago, I gloried in the thrill:
Niagara in newness! O to see
The flaked frost sparkling, shining silvery
On peach and oak, all beautifully still.

This time I would request of you, my friends.
And family, where scattered you may be
lose by, or further, even at world's ends,
To share the splendour of a Christmas tree.

Ignite with me the tapers of Advent
Three violet and one rose, each Sunday's claims,
Join in reflection on, as flickering flames
Illumine all the dark, the year just spent.

A time of thanks for opportunity
To let down roots at last. Now you may say.
Here I belong. The many years away
Have been redeemed, restored most graciously.

A call to faith and trust in One who spared
Life more than once this year. In peril's hour
Beyond all reason, logic, God has cared
Preserving for some purpose by His power.

A flash of hope, of forward look to far
Horizons and the vast expanse
Of this my Canada. We know advance
Is a *per ardua*[1] to gain our star

Let joy and gladness glow to light this day!
We toast the Sovereign, our gracious Queen:
Pay homage to the Lord, our King unseen,
Who will both bless and guide us on our way.

---

1. Latin: for arduous

SETTLED AT CHRISTMAS
KINGSVILLE; THIRD CHRISTMAS HOME

My Christmas scene: The frosted filigree
Of lace clad peach trees standing row on row
In sparkling beauty. Glorious to see
The fields fog-ridden, white with spotless snow
Fresh fallen. A full moon above the deep
Shimmer of waters, rippling in their sleep.

The daily needs: A roof, a home, a place
Where creature comforts satisfy and ease,
And art extends its charm with special grace
Of colour, form and rhythmic harmonies;
The roots of heritage, dear friends aware
Of values and concerns, of joy and care

The thought within: a gratitude of health,
For life and light; the precious gift of ways
That have not yet run out. In quiet stealth
The clock ticks on, reminder that our days
Have limits, yet give opportunity
To serve our people and community.

Recall of friends and far-flung family
Throughout our dear Dominion: urban east
Far arctic, west, Pacific...sea to sea.
Beyond the oceans! Vision is increased

To those of other lands and loyalty.
God's children all: of one humanity.

The New year comes. Dear God, give us thy peace,
Heal all our sorrow, comfort loneliness
Around the world. Let strife and warfare cease.
Provide for all, of one humanity.

The New Year comes. Dear God, give us thy peace,
Heal all our sorrow, comfort loneliness
Around the world, Let strife and warfare cease.
Provide for all, replenish emptiness.
For country and for Queen, O Lord above,
We pray to thee, for Canada, our love.

CHRISTMAS MORNING

Night wanes, Deep velvet glows
Dawn's purple; then rich rose
Illuminates the floes
Upon the lake.
No heavy ships go by:
Ice stretches far as eye
Can see. The morning sky
Has come awake.

From comfort of these walls
Would reach out everywhere
Whose embering hearth recalls
The evening fire, yet palls
At greater light...
My greeting and my prayer
Would reach out everywhere
To those for whom I care
Beyond my sight.

With grateful heart, I stand
Before thee, Lord. Thy hand
Protect our Queen and Land
This blessed morn.

> To all thy love gives gain
> For loss, and peace for pain.
> Dead hope and faith felt vain
> Arise reborn.

CHRISTMAS EVE
OXLEY BEACH

It's Christmas Eve. The flickering fire
Leaps lifelike. Shadows rise, retire
Upon the wall behind the tree
Whose coloured lights shine steadily
As stars above.

I would invoke the Christmas ghosts
Of Dickens, or the angel hosts
That rule this day. Let sound and sight
The lost through love.

A wide-brimmed boy of long ago,
A prairie schoolhouse, all aglow
With colours, candles, shining eyes
O children waiting for surprise
Of special treat,

Eight children of a family
Are grouped around a Christmas tree
With parents. Joy and happiness
Are full; as yet, time does not stress
And home is sweet.

A young man in a choir; the song
Bursts out assurance to the throng

Of worshippers; the Christ is born
Rejoice, O faithful, greet the morn
And calm your fears.

A yulebook of straw made gay
With ribboned red, from world away,
Paws at the door. Has he a place?
Do let him come. I can't erase
The alien years.

Fifth Christmas home! The fire recedes;
The tree lights hold, like love that leads
By ways uncharted yet. Love, faith
And hope we know, sufficient grace
Shall be supplied.

CHRISTMAS SNOW
BROOKSIDE REMEMBERED; HARROW

The falling snow
Drifts gently, softly down
And covers field and town.
It's Christmas time once more.
So soon? The months before
Were full of woe.

The blanket snow
Bedecks a final bed
Where I shall softly tread
To place an advent wreath
Which she, in perfect peace
Will surely know.

Amid the snow
Come carols whose refrain
Is the angelic strain.
Though life is rearranged
The stars remain unchanged
In faithful glow.

Beneath the snow
The winter wheat is green
And blossoms bud unseen
A healing quietness
Prevails. May Heaven bless
And hope regrow.

THOUGHTS
KINGSVILLE

High wind, dark clouds, cold rain!
December comes again....
No Christmas sign we see
But Main Street cheerfully
Lit up. Is there a star
For one who feels so far
Removed from joy this year?
A word of hope and cheer?

The yulebook, is here
Red ribboned, yet his sere
Straw beard displays a tear.
She's home; she celebrates
Within eternal gates,
And from that realm of light
Soft music fills the night.

God's peace! On Christmas morn
Be first in us reborn!
God's peace with one who sleeps
As well as one who keeps
Her memory in trust.
It comes! All conflicts must
In love be reconciled...
Your gift, O Holy Child.

God's glory! Thus to come
Into our world so numb
With coldness of the heart
And pride that splits apart
All the community
Created. Unity
At Bethlehem restored
Is glory to the Lord.

Good will to all mankind:
Loosed are all bonds that bind
And separate. An end
To guilt and
sorrow. Bend
Our wills to His, to start
A time of newness. Heart
Be joyful, all is well.
He comes, Immanuel

DECEMBER EVENING
AFTER WRITING JOURNEY OF PEACE

The dusk comes early at this time of year;
The world has quieted, though skies are drear:
And so we build our own environment
Enclosed by walls, the winter to prevent.

The glow of hearth! The cheerful, burning log;
Cast shadows move like phantoms in a fog.
There's warmth and comfort; music weaves its spell
To make one much and many; all is well.

Set out a bowl of milk, the hustler cheer:
He's home at last, his yulebook is here.

Tre kronor[1] yet survive, and she who gave
Those ways for me to carry on: I save
And I uphold them. Fran, for you the far
And near are joined. Your special, shining star
Comes very close tonight, and lights the way
To give this evening such a magic sway.

Somehow past Christmases long gone return
To bless and reconcile; no need to spurn
And Saland's daughter. Deck the Christmas tree
With ornament she loved, and string the lights
Green branches brought. Blue, yellow are delights

Symbolic of the gamla and the free
Who gladly honour the Nativity.

In contemplation and reflection, peace
With past and present. Let the joy increase!
The Christ whose birth we soon shall celebrate
Came to rest or, to heal, emancipate
I draw the drapes, the midnight sky to see,
Now clear, immense, with host of galaxy.
The stars are promise of a morning bright:
"Break forth, O beauteous heavenly light!"

---

1. Swedish: three crowns

CHRISTMAS JOY

"Hodie Christus natus est!"[1]
Those Christmas words, to us addressed
Bring joy to hearts that are depressed:
The sad and sorrowful are blessed.

We've waited, long to us it seemed.
But not in vain. All we have dreamed
And more has come, the glory streamed
That brought deliverance, we're redeemed.

We have known loss. The hand of death
Reached out to make our landscape less
And heavens greater. Now repress
The tears of memory and bless.

The radiance illuminates
As darkness everywhere abates,
The bitterness and pain, the hates
Of mankind in its direst straits.

Infected by the angel's song
With shepherds we are swept along.
To join adoring, thus belong
To Him who comes, in weakness, strong.

A Benedictus,[2] song of praise
To Him, the Lord of Life we raise,
With cherubs joining us, the lays
Are glories from creation's days!

Let guilt and grief be set aside.
Nor ancient rivalries divide
The gates of Heaven are opened wide:
Come Christ of peace, with us abide.

---

1. Latin: Christ is born today.
2. Latin: A blessing

IN TIME OF CHANGE

Though some things change
Essentials still remain
And Christmas comes again.

Should we feel strange
At increased distance, far
From other days? The star

That brought the eastern sages, led
Them to the crib, is still
God's symbol of good will.

Our varied needs are met and fed
By hope born of a birth
That is unique on earth

King Liberator? Mighty Lord?
We know our need. The answer, this?
A helpless child? But lest we miss

The gift's significance, accord
It but a fleeting, friendly nod.
Comes the angelic host! To God

All glory, on earth peace!
Not born of arms or violence
But through a girl's obedience.

The wonder will not cease,
And can sustain,
Make change to gain.

THROUGH CHRISTMAS INTO A NEW YEAR

The threshold year.
Or time we fear.
It's come; it's nineteen eighty-four.
Orwellian? What is in store?

Have we not made our pilgrimage
To Bethlehem, our Christ? Engage
No longer tasks of everyday
That kept us busy. Seeking pay?

We wanted much for shopping:
arms overloaded, dropping
A parcel here or there!
Yet to that Presence nearing,
Gifts started disappearing
And hands were empty. Bare!

Like refugees in need.
We could do nought but plead
For help, O Lord, from you.
We're crippled and we're blind:
We're crippled and we're blind:
No wholeness left to find
In us, but you are true.

"O fill our open hands
With blessings, break the bands
That hold us prisoner.
Give us peace and joy this hour.
Transform us with your power
To which our souls defer."

Our prayers were answered,
we were filled
As fearful hearts were strangely stilled.

So we go forth, with crib and star
As signs that Heaven is not far,
But in our midst. Emanuel
Means God is with us, all is well.

LIGHTS COMING ON
A PRAYER

The chill December rain
Beats out its own refrain:
Strange little drummer boy
Remote from Christmas joy.
Implicit tears and sadness
Erode the season's gladness.

Is this the substance,
real, yet disappointing?
In dripping dreariness is no anointing:
But homes and hearts are warm, and we
Rejoice once more at Christ's nativity.

As we light Advent candles, Christmas lights
May we be lit, illuminating nights.
Of human need,
By word and deed.
A warming fire,
of care, concern
Begins to burn.
The inner glowing,
Becomes a growing
Beyond all knowing;
Is life bestowing
And hope's desire.

And in the shining of our love,
Transmitting God's descends the Dove
Of power, peace and holiness.
So all is well. Much joy, God bless.

THOUGHTS IN SEASON

December rain
From leaden skies
To hearts and minds a heaviness implies.
To break the gloom requires an act of will,
Determined resolution. Better still
Expectant innocence of girl or boy.
Attuned to joy:
Childfaith regain.

Illuminate!
In love a light
Has come into the world to end the night;
Establish righteousness on David's throne;
Undo the power structures that now own
Our very lives and shape their destiny;
We shall be free
So celebrate.

Can Advent raise
Assenting nod
That nothing is impossible with God?
Salvation is created; East and West
May come as kings and beggars and be blessed;
Unlearn the arts of war for ways of peace.
Then never cease
Our song of praise.

A healing time!
The crippled walk.
The blinded see, the dumbly silent talk.
Relationships that came unstuck, unglued,
Bound up in love, in peace can be renewed.
Such is your power, wonderfully mild.
O holy child
And Lord sublime.

REFLECTIONS ON CHRISTMAS

It's Christmas time. The year has made its round
Through seasons sequenced, waxing, we glance to forward waning.
Another year is gone! There is profound
Awareness of continued change, restraining
The festive mood with memories.
And outlook with uncertainties.

Yet change is more than an effacement:
For loss, the young can be replacement.
Match backward glance to forward look!
Then upward, opening the book
For the story of old
Still new when retold.

Thus Luke's account is very rich
In heavenly choice of cast. With which
Can one identify? The older set?
That priestly couple, shepherds, crowd.
The wise men (scientists, if I'm allowed!)
Plus others, even older yet:
The rapt and patient sentinel
Who waited, saw Emmanuel.

For those afield at night
The dark glowed strangely bright

With tidings of great joy.,
The words of Simeon
Who held the promised one
We also may empty.
Accept release
In gift of peace.

And all is well.

HOMELESSNESS

At Christmas time we celebrate God's homelessness.
A paradox: we shut him out
To our distress.

Birth took from him
The warm and sheltering envelope of Mary's body
Safeguarding growth to form:
The fruit housed by the shell.

As Christ, God came to dwell
Among us, yet was not received.
"The foxes have their holes, each bird its nest.
But I am without place my head to rest"
So spoke the Lord unwanted
In this the world he made.

The troubler and the unbelonger,
The healing, loving vagrant, never still
Or silent, got his geared to income housing
High on a hill.
A cross. They nailed him fast, to die:
And at the last
A stone – blocked tomb.

Homeless, he built for us a city
With twelve gates and foundations.

OF TIME AND CHRISTMAS

Engrossed in our affairs
And daily work and cares
We are taught unawares
When Christmas signs appear.

So we are disarrayed
More than a bit dismayed
With patience, tempers frayed:
Already, end of year?

How has the year gone by
Left what to dare and try
As clouds on shifting sky:
So much remains undone

There is an urgency
As time runs out, as we
In our closed system, see
An end, for us no sun.

Then Christmas comes: O holy night:
When love and life brought forth new light:
Beyond our expectation bright
It calms the anxious heart.

Hence double nature of our calendar
The Christian, and the regular:
The end of year is secular
But sacred Advent is a start.

The eager eyes of children playing
Confront us with the ancient saying:
"Except you be like these, displaying
Sweet innocence, you have no place."

And that is part of mercy, though severe:
As we relinquish things held dear
Eternal clarities appear
And we become aware of grace.

IN CONVERTENDO
LATIN: IN CONVERTING. SEE PSALM 126

Last Christmas, just a year ago
Who would have thought, or dared to dream
Of what has come, events that seem
To change the world we've come to know?

How many yearned and hoped and waited
Decades of years. Lived not to see
A frozen world of ice made free,
Inhabitants emancipated?
Are Holy Russia
Saint Michael and Saint George? The angel's knight,
Are Holy Russia's patrons. England's might
Derives alike from them. East, West
Are thus by them divinely blest.
A sigh: Change mail to business suits
Worn soberly by settlers of dispute;
Unsaint them both, as mortals plain ...
Amazingly the names remain.

O *Restitutor Orbis*,[1] Lord Divine!
Thoughts come of Cyrus. Innovator
Czar Alexander, Liberator ...
Another such, the Third in line?

Advent: incoming; *Avenir*[2]
The future, *Zukunft*,[3] now, is here.
Desired for cycles, to appear
Without war's violence of fear?

Is it for real? In Babylon
The captive felt the bonds give way
And Jacob favoured. Glorious day
With hope reborn, new world begun!

---

1. Latin: Restorer of the world
2. French: Future
3. German: Future

SWEET FRAGILE SOUNDS

Another year, and how to celebrate?
Alive and well, we seek to integrate
Our gratitude, and are not unaware
Of change: Deliverance where Long awaited
Is matched by loss, as if our kind is fated
To conflict, Are we then beyond repair?

So much diminished: our world that teemed
With every form of life, until it seemed
Just inexhaustible: whose oceans gleamed
With silver scales and fins, while land and air
Were full of creatures beautiful and fair.
So much is gone to waste, exterminated.
O, could the mess we made be mitigated!
Could all start over? What can be redeemed?

Contrast the comfort and security
Of fireside at Christmas with the tree
Decked out in ornaments of many years,
With larger setting loved: it shakes as if
The nation teeters, at an edge, a cliff?
The centre fails, uncertainty breeds fears.

And suddenly rise fragile, exquisite
Sweet sounds: Gesu Bambino.[1] Hope re-lit
Illuminates the dark, restoring faith
In tidings of great joy. The Promise stands
Until encompassing our world, all lands;
Renewing us, assuring Peace and Grace.

---

1. Italian: Baby Jesus

BE NOT AFRAID

Angelic words! They set at ease
Minds stricken by uncertainty
When empires fall in agony:
And troubles rock economies.

They touch our fears most personal;
Of ageing, weakness, failure, death
That closes in with every breath:
While pain and illness come to all.

Though first addressed to priest and maid.
Then shepherds with their flocks by night
Accompanied by glorious light;
These words of joy to all relate.

Responding. We take heart, made free
Of inner bonds that sore afflict,
Like chains that hobble and restrict:
Self captives set at liberty.

Not with the courage of despair.
Or disciplined philosophy:
Here is universality
Good news for people everywhere.

And not to humankind alone,
But to all creatures, great and small
Spreads One who mourns each sparrow's fall
And hears the planet's ceaseless groan.

HARD TIMES AND CHRISTMASES

It's Christmas, year's end, bottom line:
Accountants add, create, define;
The answers are all there:
We hear a maiden's song again.
Plant layoffs never cease

The bottom line today is that!
The hungry still increase,
Plant layoffs never cease;
Ideal efficiency
Is only misery

Bank instabilities
With high-rise bankruptcies,
Junk bonds and leverage.
At bottom of the page.
No balance is achieved:
Have we not been deceived?

The Lord of the Magnificat
Is one who sets things straight
Receiver at the gate.
His justice wrings out wrong
As hailed in Mary's song.

The hungry filled. The meek.
Meek Exalted, raised the weak.
The last shall come in first
The arrogant dispersed.
The wealthy are opposed.
The mighty ones deposed .

Come Lord, come heavenly Christmas light,
Illumine all our troubled night:
Thy Kingdom through ourselves deploy:
Redeemed by love to peace and joy.

LET HOPE RETURN

An end to lengthening light:
The solstice brings bright
Festivities since ancient times
To those who live in northern climes.
With Christmas grafted on the heavenly light
We add to day the radiant holy night.

This year has seen recovery of sight
And yet, not all the seeing brings delight:
The world of weal and woe still presses
Into our lives: at times depresses
Our spirits with its dark refrain:
Injustice, violence and pain.

As those of old, the minute's gain
Of sunshine can the hope sustain
That spring will come, and life prevail
With love and warmth. Let hope avail
Itself of sign in dark of night
Except an in-break of the light
At every level humanly
As known to us; All doubt will flee.
We read again the Christmas story;
And celebrate its joy and glory.

AND STILL COMES

December such uncertainty!
The old reliability
Around about, seems gone and lost
As if some hard November frost
Had ended life and trust in men;
Desertified, made alien.

And even where good sense prevails
By margins minuscule, avails
Such narrowness to heal divides?
Search the familiar; what abides?
What fruitful land has not been sold
And Midas-style, turned into gold?

We yearn for something that remains
And constant value still retains.
Behold the Christmas mystery!
They tell us where eternity
Come down among us, chose to dwell
In human form – Emmanuel.

Ah, but we fixed! that very fast!
Hung on a cross, he breathed his last!
But no — we lost the power to hill....
He comes! The everlasting will
Undoes the darkness of the hour;
Come Lord, your Love is peace and power.

Venite!

CHRISTMAS POEMS 1996-2010

Victor and Margaret

RETURN TO JOY
1996

The Christmas message spoken then
Is timeless still; and so again
It says it's not by power or might,
But by the spirit that makes right.
Count not on high degree, the filled,
Nor the ambitious iron-willed.

That message says a heavenly NO
To all those powers we've come to know
This century of violence.
Assured destruction was defence?
Huge armies, war economies
Assured prosperity and peace.

Is bigger better?
Take this letter!
Where "Royal Mail" take a day,
Fast centralized will send astray.

We have "economies of scale"
That were prescribed, and ever fail.
We must be big. Push on until we get
To "information highway," internet
And other forms of progress set
To crash in time. Lest we forget!
Let Someone pull the plug?

O for a friendly human hug!
Come, halt to sing a carol, kneel
Before The Child, the One, and feel
Empty when ambitions cease;
Emmanuel is here, brings peace.

REBORN
1997

Now set aside the systems that control
Our daily lives, and liberate the soul
By celebrating the great gift Divine
The root of Jesse, David's royal line.

But what is monarchy today?
By revolutions blown away.
In century of violence
Destruction without precedence.
The child newborn
Seems most forlorn.

The academics may
Their prejudice display
Church moderators say
It never was this way.
The powers in armed array
Deny this breaking day.

Let all that be!
Come, let us see
The gift proclaimed
By angels named
As Saviour, Lord.
God's love out-poured
Will be adored.
It breaks the sound,
Makes systems end
And all knees bend.

Redeem, renew! Let Christmas morn
Show hope and joy again reborn.

Christmas picture of Victor and Margaret
Caption May the joy and peace of Christmas be with you today and always

CONTRASTS
1998

It's Christmas time, again, no doubt

One can't escape the secular
The reindeer stuff spectacular
Of red-nosed Rudolf and the elves;
The malls are brightly lit to pull
The customers with wallets full
Of credit cards to clear the shelves.

Is this then what it's all about?

What is the celebration's cause?
Uneasily we stop and pause:
Tradition of two thousand years?
Stock market frenzy manifest
Will presently our patience test
And yet, beneath, a truth appears.

Identified is holy Ground
Ignore the litter, sweep aside
The trash, the commerce, seeking ride
On birthday of the Prince of Peace.
For time is breached; Eternity
Divine has touched humanity,
And light through love effects release.

Let joyful, thankful songs abound.

These tidings transform everything!
Impel some kind of offering.

We feel the pain of emptiness.
But there is nothing we can give;
All that we have is negative;
We blew our treasures, we confess.

Come soon, O Lord; bring change profound.

NOT ALONE
1999

Is there a word to share
That speaks to fear and care?

Just sixty years ago the King faced fear
In wartime Christmas. What of the New Year
In halting speech, described it as a gate;
Full of uncertainty. It was too late
To turn around; he urged we place our faith
In the sustaining Hand of waiting Grace.

Today the fear is degradation
Of earth, of oceans, forests, all creation
We need for life. It is the misery
Of Better life through chemistry.
It isn't faithful prophets spreading gloom;
Ecologists predict our certain doom.

Our churches hurt, for compromise
Has silenced truth, confused the wise.
When hymns of faith are modernized
To jingles, we are not surprised.
Clear words of truth, with meaning unalloyed
Political correctness has destroyed.
We count Millennium
And wonder what will come.

The gate of time! Our Christmas gift, which came
As Word divine, Emmanuel the name.
Who joined his creatures, made his humble dwelling
Among them, darkness with great light dispelling
The Lord of Time, who stands at New Year's gate.
To take our hand, and make the crooked straight

Unchanged is he, true, steadfast as of old
He is our guide, whatever may unfold.

REFLECTIONS
2000

Through the door a bit ajar
I see the *Samovar*....
Where are the places it has been?
What are events that it has seen?

It left the land where it was made
Lived rurally, suburbanly.
It moved and moved; it was displayed,
A treasure of the family.

Some eighty Christmases was part
Of home and life, of hope and heart.
First time we say two thousand year
And still it greets with silver cheer.

Call us to again to celebration
For Advent given every nation!

To mankind doomed, as sailors caught
Beneath the sea, for us is wrought
Deliverance from hopelessness,
In form of child of righteousness.

As *Samovar* is used and drained
Of gift to us, the child retained
None of its awesome power, but gave
Its very life a world to save.

That truth abides, remains unchanged;
That Love still summons the estranged;
The Word of Christmas, Life and Light.
Makes doubt and darkness strangely bright.

HEALING
2001

Friends, family, and all who came our way
As guests, who brought joy from far away.
It seems but yesterday we sent our greetings far;
Reflecting Christmas thoughts around a *samovar*;
The contrast of the vessel that had served
The changing family; was still intact, preserved.

> Where went the time? A year has gone.
> It made its mark. Much came undone.
> From friend who died on Christmas day;
> From illness, pain that seemed to stay;
> Afflictions touching lives held dear
> Uncertainty that would not clear.

> Not only touching individual
> Existence; Life in general.
> A dark September morning's madness
> purged our complacency, brought sadness:
> Invoking war and violence.
> Where will it end? Is there defense?

And yet, we heard Kim Phuc, once napalmed child .
In and through her a war is reconciled;
In freedom, love, forgiving's special grace
Drawn from the wellspring of her Christian faith.
Like her, the wisemen, and the shepherds, we
Adore the new born Lord, and healed, made free .

CELEBRATION
2002

Thanks be to Thee
O Lord of Love!
From Heaven above
You came to be
With us, to live
And life to give.

And so we bring our tears of loss
For dear departed ones, here gone;
In faith believing that not one
Is lost, but resting, lives in you.
This is our faith, the word is true;
In you they flourish, crown from cross.

The world is full of violence
As evil draws its consequence;
Afflicting all you made and gave
Creation groans to you to save.

Truth will prevail, and every knee
In earth and heaven shall bend to Thee.

    Great joy makes sorrow cease
    God's glory is our peace.

ADVENT PRAYER
2003

Come in, O Lord, we wait for you!
That was the hope of Israel.
Desire of prophets who were true
To calling faithful, to foretell
The vision of a Kingdom, new;
Of peace and joy, with all things well.

We greatly need your healing touch!
Anticipate the Kingdom Age
When righteousness will be in power.
That earth respond in fruitfulness:
Salvation comes, with grace to bless.
For human strength, this is too much
Here greater power must engage.

Two thousand years ago, you came
To break the bonds and set men free
Gave us the power of the Name
Set captives all at liberty.

Disciples asked you: "Lord, O when?
Will you restore the earth and bring
The Kingdom in?" You said not then,
But soon, assured. So come, O King!
Two thousand years, our need is great:
The world seems in a hopeless state.
We need your truth, your justice, light!
The wholeness promised: all made right!

Thy Kingdom come!

AGAIN IT'S CHRISTMAS
2004

It's Christmastime again.......
Is it a year already since we sent
Our Christmas greetings? As they went
We wondered what the year ahead
Would bring. Would hold of good and dread.

A time of sadness......
Dear friends of years have passed away
And illness must be kept at bay
War, violence, the world divide.
And good traditions are denied.

A time of thanksgiving
There has been healing when we prayed
We thank the Lord for Love displayed.
For caring family and friends.
For all on which life depends.

A time of joy.......
When glory touched us by surprise
With happiness, to realize
How good the days have been, in spite
Of much still waiting to be right.

A time for prayer
The Gift Divine, The Word endures
It is the Promise that assures.....
Thanks be to God; hope is reborn
For peace, good will each Christmas morn.

ADVENT PRAYER
2005 - MATTHEW 1:21

The year winds down and Christmas comes;
Time to reflect and count up sums
Of joys and sorrows, near and far:
To lift up eyes, and see the Star.
And heed its message; celebrate
The birth of Him whom God calls great.

The memories of war long past,
Of death, destruction, carnage vast,
This anniversary year,
Were matched to changes, threats to dear
And precious ones, to health and lives.
Much has been lost, yet much survives.

And so we join the magi, bring
Ourselves as only offering
Before the child born to be King
And King forever. Everything
Is His to save, to heal and free;
We worship him, eternally.

TOUCH OF A HAND
2006 - FOR MARGARET

Again I take your hand in mine
As I did often, also here
To warm the chill, a simple sign
Of love, and care, and inner cheer.

If I could pass my strength to you,
So bridge the union of our touch,
I'd see the colour show a new
Bright warmth that could restore so much!

Or draw the pain from you to me
Through these linked hands, that could relieve
Your hurt, make you feel whole and free!
There's One who can, that we believe.

The one who touched the garment's hem
Not only healed, but daughter named!
By Jesus, Saviour, Nought could stem
The flow of power her faith had claimed.

As she was healed, she worshipped him
Who stopped the pain, the flow, the loss;
Had she awareness, although dim
That he would take it to the Cross?

CHRISTMAS THOUGHTS
2007

What shall I write, what say that would apply
To Christmas in this quiet and lonely year?
I read Luke 2 again and found the field
Where Shepherds watched, saw winter darkness yield.

To angel's brightness, hear the "Do not fear"
And joyful tidings, saw the host appear
To sing their threefold song to God, Earth, Man.
A pattern to my pruner's total span.

Glory to God
God has reached out to lost humanity
Emmanuel will set all people free.
In David's town a Saviour has been born
Go find him in a crib, this blessed morn.

And Peace on Earth:
Let violence, let strife and warfare cease:
On crowded urban streets, let there be peace.
Let it begin in home and families,
Go on to churches and communities.

Good will to men:
Intent is healing to all humankind;
Walk upright for the lame
The hungry fed, the homeless shelter find
God's Spirit clears, repairs, the darkened mind.

This Christmas wish . . . tall order to fulfill
And yet, with God, there's no impossible.

TIDINGS IN TROUBLED TIMES
2008

When money markets tumble
Great banking houses crumble;
As values shrink, and homes are lost
The price of greed is human cost

We ask, why did the government
Not act, this meltdown to prevent?
Can't they somehow the world repair?
So Christmas finds us, unaware.

Like those afield, who watched their sheep
Like we our assets, seek to keep
All that we can. Then sudden light
Of Heaven shines with Glory bright

An Angel of the Lord appears
Proclaims great joy, and calms all fears
Announces then the Saviour's birth
For all the people of the earth.

The in-break of eternity
With blessing, power to set us free
Brings hope and peace that will restore.
With shepherds, magi, we adore.

CHRISTMAS RESTORES
2009

"The happy Christmas comes once more
The heavenly guest is at the door..."

What better way
Is there to say
What this sweet Danish carol sings?
Good times or less
Joy or distress
It's time to greet the King of kings.

A year this was of much uncertainty
The economic crisis grew, then eased
As massive measures spurred activity
Were stimuli effective? If they ceased,
Would things get worse? Hard times are personal
As anyone who's been laid off can tell.

We are the people who in darkness walk
Confronted by life's problems everywhere;
With media's incessant doomsday talk
Inviting, tempting us to black despair.
We halt in our confusion, feel and grope
And long for any sign of life and hope.

And then comes Christmas and the lights come on
That shine in darkness, take us to the field
Where angels came, and Heaven's glory shone,
While tidings of great joy were there revealed
To simple shepherds, of the Saviour's birth,
With "Glory in the Highest; peace on earth."

A DREAM OF CHRISTMAS DAY
2010

Was it a vision or a dream?

Bright sunlight shining on clean snow
Fresh fallen, wintering the fall;
By star and sun is nature's show
Of welcome to the Lord of all.

"Get in," the Driver said to me;
"I am to show you needs that cry."
The seatbelt snapped obediently,
The engine purred; the town flashed by.

En route downtown, beneath a bridge
Were cardboard boxes, homeless stays;
They beg at doors of privilege
Of commerce on all business days.

Then came an urban hospital,
Where science serves the best of care;
Yet what of cancers terminal,
Crash victims, strokes and dark despair?
Passed houses, arrayed festively
With pain beneath the greenery;
A corner church where reverently
Are people blessed abundantly.

Car stops; I'm back. Whence came that creche?
The Driver smiles. "You saw the need
For Saviour King; the Word made flesh
Go worship Him in faith and deed!"

Thy Kingdom come. Thy will be done.

FAMILY PHOTOS

The Dirks family. Family photos were an important part of family life and family gatherings. Standing, left to right: Victor, Elisabeth, Neil, Rosemarie, Henry, Irene, John. Seated: Alexander, Marguerite, Agnes.

A more formal family photo at a studio. Standing (l-r): Neil, Rosemarie, Victor, John, Marguerite, Henry. Seated: Agnes, Elisabeth, Alexander, Irene.

A later formal family photo. Standing (l-r): Irene, Victor, Marguerite, Neil, Rosemarie, Henry. Seated: John, Agnes, Alexander, Elisabeth.

An informal family photo taken at Marguerite's home. Standing (l-r): Elisabeth, Neil, Victor, John, Henry, Marguerite. Seated: Rosemarie, Agnes, Alexander, Irene.

Victor with his first wife, Frances

Victor and his parents, Alexander and Agnes Dirks

Victor and his second wife, Margaret Barton

EASTER SONNETS

GOOD FRIDAY 1975

Good Friday: silence; the precipitate
Confusion of retreat, the hue and cry
Of legions disarrayed in fear, for nigh
Has come the hour they must evacuate
This lovely land they sought to dominate -
Be gone, ye warhawks, rebels, haste to fly.
Abandon arms and flags, who God defy
Must yield to judgment most commensurate,
The freed are dazed. Who will materialize
Amid these trees, these fields; this beach secure
To breakers white—capped, like a beating heart?
Their steady drumming gives a rhythmic part
To piping in the woods. The overture
Is underway; recovered is the prize.

HOLY SATURDAY 1975

We look, we wait; in worry we confess
Our doubts and fears; the deep uncertainty.
The enemy has flown, and left us free:
Unchained, unshackled, but with no redress.
Why freedom now? We know the merciless
Brute adversary gave no liberty
From goodness of his heart. Strange victory:
Consolidating it means to possess.
In lofty landscape lately tyrannized,
Delay must not be long. There is expectancy
Of hope in those so recently assailed;
Who know that when the foe retreats, prevailed
Must have the royal cause. What urgency!
The mighty, shattered, yield to the despised.

EASTER 1975

We seek a king; a conqueror of might
Who breaks the spear, and renders desolate
All earthly power: republic, nation, state;
Before whose presence brave men take to flight;
Abandon banners and all tools of fright;
Tear off their uniforms; leave desolate
Their missiles, cannon, magazines of hate;
To seek, but find no refuge from the light.
Then *You* come walking, whole, advance through strife
Into our midst. We gaze, we sense, we know
Yours is the world, the universe and all.
The sons of war, the evil killers fall
Into their master's darkness: death below
We hail your victory, O Lord of Life!

EASTER IN ONTARIO, 1978

The winter's snow recedes where drifts stood high,
Green grass peeks out, half fearful, yet half bold.
The tiny spears of crocuses unfold,
And buds begin to swell. The clearing sky
Is dotted with returning birds who cry
Their welcome. Ice still stretches, but its hold
Will soon give way to water, and the cold
Of winter will not long the sun defy.
All these are symbols of eternal hope?
So we are told, and yet we doubt and grope.
Then Easter comes! O risen Lord, your light
Breaks in and banishes all fear and fright.
Your radiance blesses. Open hands extend
The proof of life. All doubts are at an end.

25 March 1978; after a hard winter

EASTER 1982

Like earth, let heart respond
To warmth and sun. Beyond
The April storms and snow
The grass is green; the show
Of early buds sustains
The faith of spring. Remains
To us to honour, meet
The Lord of all to greet.

The glory of the day
Belongs to him whose sway
Is infinitely great;
And yet, he shares his state
And triumph. There is room
For all to join. The gloom
Is gone; the crooked, square
In marvelled morning fair.

The matrix of our hurts
He lovingly inverts
A rod makes the product one
In *Unum Deum*.[1] Gone
Are all the little pains,
Our fears of losses, gains
Beyond our own control:
O springtime of the soul!

He comes, alive, to claim
Death's own. *Invoke The Name*;
No curse can then afflict,
Nor anger, joy restrict.
There are no bondsmen here;
Not dread or any fear.
Peace comes. What else could be?
God's son has made us free!

---

1. Latin: one God

WEDDING POEMS

Dedicated to my young friends
Who have brought me joy

-Victor A. Dirks, Kingsville

WHITE OAK ROAD BRIDE

Will you get dressed at home, upstairs, the way
Of white oak brides upon their wedding day?
I used to see your room. How exquisite
The style of books and dolls in lacy white!

You'll see a pair of crutches used one spring
For ankle injury at track. Small thing
Of many in your high school grades, the mix
Of study and athletics; from age six
Your daily life. In size and mind you grew
Each year, from little girl. There were so few
Times that we shared before the child cocoon
Burst open: gorgeous woman came too soon?

You'll sense the presence of your animals
Who occupied the barn; you fed your pals.
The horses that you rode; they recognize
The bride as one with them: Each life is prize
To love and cherish, share as God advise;
He called them into being; you likewise.
They bless you on this very special day,
As their dear princess, queen, this month of May.

You see that picnic table on the lawn?
Recall of summer supper; you had on
Just shorts and parted top. A big protest
From father: "Why, no girl of mine! Divest
Herself like that?" Display her merchandise?
You blushed and bit your lip at the surprise
Of belly button, midriff skin decried.
You changed; I hope you never, ever cried.

Most fair in white, all bridally arrayed
Now sweep downstairs, in radiance unafraid.
We family and friends are here to show
All of our love; to kiss you as you go.

VAD, April 24, 90
To Paula Driedger, for her Wedding Day
May 5, 1990

TO CAROL

Dear daughter of a friend, as you prepare
To marry, decked in wedding glory fair;
What words are there to let you know
That all our blessings with you go?

Remember while you wait here, stand:
The meadowlarks still sing
Down on the prairie land
As they have every spring
Since you, a crocus of the May,
Came forth to life that joyful day,
Your mother's carol, hymn of praise
For the Creator's wondrous ways.

We see you radiant in your wedding dress,
And tremble as we think of times of stress
And shadows that assailed. How doubly dear
Are you, restored, redeemed! The youth of fear,
Of darkness touching down, is set aside;
Life has prevailed, and let you be a bride.

Now is the fulness of maturity,
What then was hope. The surety
Of faith goes with you down the aisle.
The music sounds! Turn fleetingly to smile
At parents, friends, for this is no farewell
But a fulfillment. Come, all will be well.

To Carol Lark Braun on her wedding day, May 14, 1988
VAD/ May 2, 1988

WEDDING THOUGHTS

The special way you met
And then were reunited!
Whoever could forget?
One came as guest, invited
To dinner, among friends, both old and new;
The other as supporting family
Which caring sisters want to do.
Faint stirring, hopes, were verily
The substance of impossibility.

I once referred to probability
With Hassid friends, got a reproving glance:
"Do you not know that nothing is by chance?"
As Einstein put it, aptly nice:
"The Lord of Heaven plays no dice."
So in our eyes, and in God's sight
Your partnership is good and right.

If God be for you, then
We raise no questions when
The evidence is there;
The special makes aware.
At times we meditate,
And prayerfully wait;
But at this feast day great
Rejoice and celebrate!

The One who did not stint
At Cana ... mother's hint
Was confidence of special power ...
Is with us now to bless this hour.
Response He gives is generous: the fount
Of wine is goodness. Quality, amount
As then, is ever overflowing
Joy, hope and love, deep peace bestowing.

VAD, 20 July 1990. To Wesley and Elaine
on their wedding day.

GINA

How have I waited for this wedding day!
At last it's here; in springtime and in May.

Why did so many see impediments?
Disparities were magnified offence?
Do background, age, or children raise a why?
You've earned the Blessing; Let no one deny!

For longest roads still have an end
Where goals are gained, and troubles mend;
And we have come to church to celebrate
To greet you at the door, in festive state.

It's strange to see you in a dress
A transformation, we confess!
But for this day you'll do no less.
Jeans, pants and shorts you wear, possess
Exclusively. They do project
Great courage, sense which I respect
Which held your family together
As single parent braved the social weather.
Despite the pressures, you stood tall
Kept fit by playing racquetball.

And God provided; gave you this young man
Who offered you his love, himself, and lent
New vision, hope, when all had come apart.
The scars, the pain, the past did not prevent
Your saying yes once more to life, again;
Let marriage restore the wounded heart.

Your two—piece satin dress in white
With walking skirt is rather tight;
Confining to a girl who strides.
Today accept the style of brides!
The crown of flowers in your hair
Accents your beauty, youthful, fair.

May joy be yours! You've found a faith
In twin with love. May this day's grace
Be the foundation of a bond
For all of life, fruit far beyond.
For you and yours, may Happiness
Glow now and always. God will bless!

To my dear friend, Gina Bond Oltean, on her
wedding day.
May 14, 1988.
VAD.

SPECIAL OCCASION POEMS

GOD USES WHO HE CHOOSES

They were collecting taxes in those days
As now, so then. More revenue to raise
Was purpose and intent. Long wars had drained
Imperial treasury. Debt burden pained
The Roman peace. Great building plans on hold
Would start again when sparked by payment gold.

Some civil servant cunningly suggested
That Rome could extract more from the detested
Sly stiff-necked Jews and nearby Syrians
Who traded with the East, the Parthians
Where they had relatives. The puppet king
Had best cooperate in everything.

Sure that the wealth these minions estimated
Exceeded what had been anticipated.
By Pompey and by Caesar; they suggested
That effort in a census be invested.
Count one and all, not just each adult man
But women, children. Implement the plan!

To best control these people, have them go
Each to their long time base, their presence show
To the enumerators, careful scribes
Who know their families and ancient tribes

List all the property they own or claim;
Identify them by the grandsire's name!

And so the order issues forth, and goes
To town and country. Joseph has to close
His shop; be off to Bethlehem to sign
With all the others of King David's line.
Best this be quick; with Mary's pregnancy
The count could else another human see.

THE LORD OF HISTORY

Political corruption, rampant greed
Of cash-strapped governments in fiscal need
To build vast monuments to celebrate
The power of ruler greatness of the state.

    In such an opulence, who could foresee
    Decline and fall, inherent destiny?

Augustus Caesar, sitting on his throne
These routine orders signing; had he known
That he was setting up the earthly stage
F or the great drama that would end his age;

    That would replace the dynasty, and break
    Established order in relentless wake?

The symbol of the utmost cruelty
Of Rome, the cross! One day, for all to see
It would rise over Rome and Pantheon
Take over all the city, world. The one
Whose birth these orders would locate and place
Would make the empire kingdom of his grace.

The tax crazed census made the prophecy
Of Micah fit, made Bethlehem the key
Of God's salvation, to the very ends
Of earth, and time. What leadership intends
And can achieve has limits. Men propose,
Not always theirs the outcome to dispose.
Augustus served God's purpose, as did all
The Roman structure, soldiers at the call
Of power, collaborators, slaves and on.
They could not know, else might have left undone
What in their arrogance they brought to be;

    The coming of the Lord of history.

VAD March 8, 1998
In those days there went forth a decree from
Caesar Augustus…Luke 2:1

UNCERTAIN TIMES WITH CERTAINTY

Beneath a Christmas tree with ornament
Set up for services of Swedish *jul*
A quarter century, the Christmas light
Embraces good things Mennonite.

A year that brought no peace, but still the war
That tore apart the country, and the hearts
Of those who cared; of leadership that gave
Its very best in an attempt to save.

Had you prevailed, O senator, who cared!
Much deeply have the wounds cut, as unspared
The country lurched; domestic anger flared
In never ending agony despaired.
A country had a choice: the man of peace
Will not be leading.

Again a Christmas tree; a time of cheer
As friends assemble; all that we hold dear
Is joined and held.

BIRTHDAY CELEBRATIONS

A year of joy; of gifts that came
Through effort that erased the shame
Of goals mirage like moving evermore
Like life itself; the other shore.

A father's birthday! His the years
That Moses noted, where the strength
Of person can extend the length
Of days of blessed work and toil
Ere yet infirmities will spoil
The style of being free of fears.

HUBERT

They tell me you have passed away;
A mass was said last Saturday;
Remembrance, requiem, rest...
The memories are blessed
And fitting to your call,
The temple words recall.

Nunc dimittis servum tuum [1]

My own recall of you
Is Oxley Beach; the view
Of lake and water stretching far away
Beyond; your eyes saw further yet.
Far past the ships, the spike of Put-in-bay.
To what horizons? Hours seemed to forget
Your presence, meditating,
Reflective, liberating.
Was this the feeling as you sensed
The vigil greatly recompensed?
Depart; no further need,
The sentry may concede.

Secundum verbum tuum in pace

For you I played the Passion of Saint John
By Bach. So may the little angel guide
You safe to Abraham's bosom. Wide
Be gates and passages. Well done!
Your eager eyes beholding
Salvation's grace unfolding.

Quia viderunt oculi mei salutare tuum

Tannhauser like, you went to Rome;
Hope burned.
But you returned.
And all was lost: no longer home
In your Basilian order. Priest.
By own request from vows released.
Kept up the search, alone, apart,
With courage and no loss of heart.

Quod parasti ante faciem populorum

Not secret knowledge, *gnosis,*
Which openness forecloses;
Your concepts and philosophy
With intellectual integrity,
Were special gifts you shared with friends
And students, even critics. So amends
Were made for educational defects,
And wisdom gained some new respects.

Lumen ad revelationem gentiam

You stood for truth and principle;
A teacher in the great tradition;
Saint Basil's still, by your volition
In glory radiant and invincible.

Et gloriam plebis tuae Israel

Dear Lord, you cannot yet
Dismiss your servant, let him go.
Except he see your Christ. Salvation
Come to all people, and creation
Restored by word of promise; let
The votive candles glow
Our prayers expressing
And creed confessing.

Vade in pace![2] Without grieving;
Veni in pace![3] The retrieving
In your deliverance restored:
Be ever priest of Christ the Lord.

Sacerdotus in aeternam
Secundum ordinem Melchisedech[4]

To the memory of Hubert Pocock, Brasilian.

---

1. The interspersed Latin lines in this poem are taken from the Song of Simeon in Luke 2:29-32 from the Latin Vulgate translation. Translated into English in the New Revised Standard Version they are as follows:
    'Master, now you are dismissing your servant
    in peace, according to your word;
    for my eyes have seen your salvation,
    which you have prepared in the presence of all peoples,
    a light for revelation to the Gentiles
    and for glory to your people Israel.'
2. Go in peace.
3. Come in peace.
4. An eternal priest according to the order of Melchizedek

TRUST

PSALM 23:4 - IN MEMORY OF JOHN R. WARKENTIN - 2
MARCH 2005

O sudden shock of emptiness!
As when a storm blew down a pine
Last fall, and made the landscape less
For wounded space; of loss a sign.

We're grateful for your years, your life,
Where gentleness was never weak;
The loving care you gave your wife,
In health and sickness, was unique.

In family and church you showed
Great loyalty to heritage;
Maternal blessing had bestowed
Those values free of change or age.

Our generation is bereft
Of predecessors; all are gone.
We cousins have survived; you left,
The first to go, whose days were done.

Proceed in peace, and greet those dear
Who've gone before to be with God.
The Shepherd's presence casts out fear
Through comfort of his staff and rod.

210 Cheriton Ave, the family home in Winnipeg, in winter

210 Cheriton Ave in summer

A HOUSE REMAINS

A house and home for half a century!
What memories
Are harmonies
In papered walls and opening doors!
How many feet have walked its floors:
Four generations in a family.

A house that has known flowers all about
From spring through fall
And spruce trees tall
Brought by a son. The lilac burst
Of bloom each year was but the first
To gladden hearts, and cheer the goers-Out.

A house that has a Christmas dedication
In pristine snow
When bright lights glow
To welcome comers-home from near
Or far, to join at table's cheer
Once more complete the round in celebration.

VAD
7/9/88

Familienheim

Ein Heim, ein liebes Haus!
Halb ein Jahrhundert hält
Es stand der Aussenwelt.
Durch diese Türen gingen ein und aus
Die Eltern, Kinder. Ist wo Spur geblieben
In dieser Räume Stille? Leben, Lieben
Hat Nachklang immerfort
In Burg und Heimatort.

In Sommerkleid, das Haus
Umringt von Grün, bewacht
Von Blüten, Farbenpracht!
Entstammt von hier nicht manch ein Blumenstrauss
Der Kranke, Alte, Einsame erfreute
Und Hoffnung frühlingsgleich erneute?
Aus Sonnenschein und Regen
Kam Üppigkeit und Segen.

Ein Haus im Winterschnee
Mit weihnachtlicher Pracht
Hat festlich sich gemacht
Heimkehrer zu begrüssen. Fühlt wer Weh
Für schöne Tage, Gaben der Vergangenheit?
Trost bleibt die Engelsbotschaft: Freudigkeit.
Vom Christfestlicht erhellt
Ist alles hergestellt.

VAD

HOMECOMING

Process in peace! The cross precedes
The choir that follows, all in white
That symbol of redemption leads,
With book and candle, heavenly light.

You loved to sing: "We plow the fields,
And scatter seed upon the land."
As planting faith to harvest yields,
Come joyfully, with sheaves in hand.

Heed summons to a greater choir
That gathers on that distant shore
What singer would not long aspire,
To praise the Lord for evermore?

Born son of Lincolnshire, you moved
To Canada, our London here;
Cared for a mother, married, proved
Yourself in life and work career.

With church and service club, you found
Retirement years were opened wide.
Kiwanis took you all around
To places far, Pat by your side.

The years wore out the earthly tent
As said Saint Paul; a city waits,
And body new, magnificent,
To enter through its open gates.

In memory of Rupert Hilton
May 4, 1909-July 5, 2005
VAD July 6, 2005

ADVENT 2004 (PROSE)
KINGSVILLE, ONTARIO

Dear Friends and Family:

The year has gone by so quickly! A year with anxious moments as well as great joy and peace. A year of recovery; a year in which we have known amazing grace in our own lives. We are grateful to all who have cared for us during the year.

One aspect of the year was an unusually cool summer here, perhaps the coolest in some 20 years. Nights were very pleasant. The main reason for the A/C was the humidity. Moisture stress was not a problem, and planted crops generally did well.

We lost two very dear friends of many years through cancer during the year, the Rev. Paul Berry and Dr. Rod Sawatsky. At Christmas we pray for Ruth and Lorna, their respective life partners of many years. We also remember all those with illness and health problems.

A long hoped for memorial was established in the Ukrainian village where I was born; a memorial to my Warkentin grandparents in the hospital they opened in 1908. Five members of the family were present. A special thank you to brother John who took care of the final arrangements. At this time when the situation in the Ukraine is very uncertain, it is evident this may have been a golden window of opportunity. The entire family contributed to this cause ... the grandparents would have been pleased.

Our own health situation has been on the mend all year and we are very grateful to those who have let God use them in healing and restoration.

Avery special appreciation of Norman's continuous support with time and travel. We are grateful to the Lord who met needs and answered prayers beyond what we were able to ask.

We must never forget our two faithful companions, Rozzie and Sunny, our Collies. Ever there, forever loving!

Health and happiness within the family and to all whose lives have touched ours! May yours be a Christmas that manifests the reality of light shining in the darkness, of a rebirth of faith and hope ... and a Happy and Prosperous New Year! As Tiny Tim says "God Bless Us All!!"

Margaret and Victor

WITNESS

When the rustling spring wind
Is singing through tall grasses
When in the sugar beet fields
One can tell the rows from the road
When the alfalfa blooms purple
And high overhead fly the gulls
Calling, crying, lost from some sea
Yet somehow always belonging

We will think of you, Jason.

Lying on the ceramic tile:
Strangely quiet, with only a rivulet
Bright red blood seeping away
Witness in the arena tradition;
Lying alone, cast into seeming silence
Never to speak again, never to pray.
Grain of wheat falling into the ground:
Dying, it flourishes greatly.

We give thanks for you, Jason.

Not the hate that pulled the trigger;
Or the demon that fed that fury;
Or the coldness of death apparent,

Nor the grave and covering earth:
Nothing whatever can separate
You from the Love of the Living Lord.
Which also embraces us in the present
And unites us with those in Eternity.

We know you are with us, Jason.

In memory, Jason Lang[1], 1982-1999
Taber, Alberta
VAD May 13 9 1999

---

1. Jason Lang was the victim of a school shooting in Taber, Alberta on 28 April 1999. Although the shooting was indiscriminate and not targeted at Lang, he succumbed to his injuries.

BIRTHDAY SALUTE

Three quarters of a century
Of life in times of destiny
Brings much to mind and memory.

My second birthday's present: You
Born brother at a time when few
In that sad land had hope anew.

As we grew up, our ways diverged
The times beset us, never splurged
But we survived, when troubles surged.

Life has been lived; if not as well
As some have known, we too can tell
Of happiness, and all is well.

With common birthday, let me share
Reflective thoughts on when and where,
Of family, and friends and care.

There may be others who can bask
In bigger things accomplished, ask
What we have done with given task.

It all depends on how we measure;
With God the little things are treasure.
Our love, our life, is at his pleasure.

Non nobis,[1] Lord; we have no claim
To preservation, status, fame.
Life is a gift; we bless your Name.

To my brother Neil on his 75th birthday
VAD on his 77th birthday
August 11, 1998

---

1. Latin: not us

ONE HUNDRED YEARS

There is a sense of awe and reverence
At such a moment, such a special day;
First for this family! What recompense
To pay the Lord, the psalmist asked, but say
The facts before the people, and proclaim
The power, the glory, and the Holy Name.

We could pick up a book of history
Of these one hundred years, when all has changed;
Where crowns and empires fell; new tyranny
And greater evil for the old exchanged.
Where airborne is the travel once on train,
And the electrons tell us there is gain.

But you should tell it. From Ukrainian town
You came as girl to work, and found the love
Of God in Christ, and a young man. The frown
Of family was bridged, and Heaven above
Poured out the blessing. War and famine years
Were left by emigrant's departing tears.

New country and new problems! How to live
And raise your gifted children? Faith came first
And that was right. War came; one learned to give
And so survive. The family dispersed

With time and chance, and yet the home assailed
By change and time, with courage still prevailed.

The years have flown, and time has had its way
With institutions, human works and more.
Beloved faces see no more the light of day;
Held in God's love, they live forevermore.
Go on in faith, in hope, in love, increase.
Love is forever, all our joy and peace.

See I Corinthians 13

To my Aunt Anastasia on her
100th birthday, Nov 16, 2000
VAD

PRESENCE

In the long night
When sleep has flown,
And in the dark
You feel alone;
With no respite
The troubled mind
Would like to find
A place to park,

But keeps on circling round the lot.
Did you not see an opening
Accommodation promising?
Or is this all forbidden zone?
What refuge, rest, needs to be shown
To one who asks if God forgot?

When time gets blurred for lack of sleep,
Exhaustion claims a watch to keep;
And so you feel impelled to drive,
As fear of impact makes you strive.

Slow to a stop; admit the One
Whom light or dark as equal face;
Slide over, let him steer you on;
As driver he will pick your place.

He's very near;
He does not hide, Stands right beside Your bed and you.
Reach out and find
His loving hand
To you inclined;
To understand
And ease your fear: Faith, hope renew.

VAD, Feb 14, 1992
To Betty Mae

ADVENT AND ALWAYS

In Advent season you were born;
As promised Christmas rose, you came.
It was a chilly winter morn
In Winnipeg; new love, nice name!

When families were large, the space
Between the generations closed.
Each child in order took its place
In service, as was then supposed.

Important matters you addressed
In youth: decisions prayerfully
Of faith, career and spouse were blessed
For life and for eternity.

Transplanted west, to Calgary,
Neath arched chinook you found your place.
In happy home, own family,
You sang your song, and there was Grace.

Reflecting back, I realize
How much I've missed; how little shared;
Beneath the cross all failure lies
With restoration well prepared.

For we relate; our heritage,
Genetic, social, is a bond
That holds in spite of stress and age;
Let distance be, we still respond.

And though we ask, where has time gone;
When years now say retirement;
With loving effort, much got done,
And more, in power of *Advent*.

To my sister Rosemarie, on her 65th birthday
Dec 3, 2002
VAD

BLESSED DEPARTURE

Depart in peace! your very eyes have seen
Salvation; in a life of hundred years.
A life that seemed more troubled than serene,
Were one to measure storms and fears.

Depart in peace! Whatever force beset
Yourself and all your sibling family
That left your homeland, needing to forget
The hunger, and the terror; you were free

Within your soul; indwelling was the Lord;
Providing refuge out and inwardly.
In Winnipeg you worked, believed the Word
And found Ontario and your destiny.

Depart in peace! You drew on heritage!
The Ewert wisdom and humility
With which your father could Machno assuage
And thus deliver a community.

Depart in peace! Let angels bear you hence.
In little things you have shown competence
The Master's joy awaits; he will dispense
Your just reward and blessed recompense.

VAD In memory of 'Tinchen Rempel
September 8, 2008

A CENTURY

A century! We celebrate a life
Of hundred years, this very day.
Begun in peaceful Waldheim, far from strife,
Long times ago, and far away,

A century of dreadful violence
Revolt and war and genocide;
Mankind's veneer stripped of pretence
When madness ruled, right was defied.

A century in which the world grew small;
Electrons now communicate.
All's globalized and changed beyond recall.
As processes accelerate.

A century of knowledge; in increase
Quite exponentially, unique;
Unlimited the thrust. The promised peace
Hangs by a thread quite frayed and weak.

Your century! You've turned one hundred years
Into a life creative, good.
A marriage, and a home, knew joy, and tears,
Raised family, did what you could.

God's century! From youth a child of faith
You knew His presence, ever true.
Today we pause, laud His Amazing Grace;
Blessed be this day; peace, joy to you!

For Catherine Rempel on her 100th birthday, May 3, 2008
VAD

ST. PAUL'S CATHEDRAL

On quiet, silent roads I drive;
Urge the great engine forward: strive
With hungry power, as if alive.
It throbs, it thrusts; I shall arrive
To share the longed-for Easter morn.
In rosy dawn, a thought is born.

    From some great deep
    The eager heart receives
    A shock of trembling sweep.
    But who believes
    This strange intelligence?
    Unsure the ear remains
    And tensely strains
    The words to sense:

    Crushed is the Usurpator;
    He comes, the Pantocrator![1]

The road runs eastward to the sun
Now rising, flaming red, upon
The clouds dispersing in the light;
A thrill of pure, unbounded sight.

Floorboard the pedal, speed, more speed!
There are still many miles that need
To pass on Highway Royal.
Then London's signs start to appear:
Imperial names, forever dear
To one devoutly loyal.

The glorious cathedral greets
The pilgrim-visitor, and meets

    The need to share
    And kneel in prayer;
    To join in celebration
    Among the congregation.

Here lost amid the caring crowd
Of worshippers, am I allowed

    To raise
    In praise
    My voice in song?

The trumpets blow, the organ swells;
Outside the ringing of great bells

    Acclaims
    Proclaims
    To all the throng:

    He is arisen!
    Our Christus Victor
    Death's Interdictor;
    Indeed arisen!

Far distant, Hallelujas rise ...
The vista opens: from the skies
Descends the angel host to greet
Their conquering champion, who defeat
Three days gone by, so recently
Transformed to total victory.

> *Destroyed the* Usurpator,
> *O glorious Pantocrator!*

This is thy triumph, Lord. No Caesar's name
Can match this moment; no one ever came
Back from the dead, from Hell and grave before;
Nor crossed the Jordan to the other shore,
And then returned. All other battles lose
Their lustre, seem but shabby cruelties.
Compared to this of total liberation
That makes an end of bondage, domination.
Before this Triumphantor, who refuse
To give their homage, sinking to their knees?

Proceed, you heralds, shout, proclaim, apprise!
Shatter you trumpets the expectant air!
Awake the slumbering earth to spring, invoke the skies
To rain redemption down, this Easter fair.

Thy standard leads the triumph in:
The cross held high; once sign of shame
Despised and shunned, but now *The Name*,
The Sign that conquers all the power of sin;
Whose greatness is nonpareil and prevails
Against all other ensigns; none avails.

A teenage maiden holds the cross
As the procession's crucifer.
One can't resist contrasting here
To hairy veterans of war's campaign
With notch marked broadswords for their slain.
Slight girl with shining eyes and toss
Of flowing hair; in purple dressed
With surplice white; the paradox

Of weakness that is strength, and mocks
Our nationality professed.

The banners follow, blue and white,
Bestitched with gold, relate to signs.
Rich coloured in the window panes,
Which faith traditional retains.

    The One True Light;
    The verdant vines;

The *Leo extribo*, the bread
Of life, the fish, the lamb of God,
The Alpha and Omega, red
The wine to signify the blood;
The mystic rose, which tints the light
Through panes enclosing sense and sight.

Somewhere the pipers blow,
While red gowned maidens show
Their skill with fife and flute,
And beauty contribute.

Two thousand years of Christendom
In this procession have become
Mixed visions of the eye and mind;
All present here, and intertwined.

    The bugles and the brass,
    The *Musika* en masse.
    With ancient harps and tympani,
    Strikes up a joyful litany
    Of airs
    Fanfares
    Arouse the throng
    To join the song.

Who can maintain a silence here
As ancient stones cry out to cheer;
The stained-glass windows quiver
As filtered light beams shiver.

    The blinding light
    Of Thee in sight!
    A thousand suns
    Are not so bright,
    Intensely white,

    We shade our eyes.

    A rustling runs
    And irresistibly
    We peek. To our surprise
    Unblinded, we may say.

He comes! In way uniquely his,
He walks; he needs no chariot or steed ,
Nor crown. The obvious has no need
To flaunt or advertise. It is.
Surrounding are the tetramorphs …
Such creatures! Winged, eyed unbelievably,
Deep minded beings inconceivably
Superior to humans. Utter dwarfs
We sense ourselves to be at all these powers;
Yet we rejoice; their Lord is also ours.

    You broke the Usurpator;
    All hail, O Pantocrator

The vaulted spaces overhead,
So empty, are now filled instead
By angel hosts with levelled spears,
Led by Saint Michael, who appears

    As mighty leader
    And special pleader

For God's own people: Israel
And all believers since as well.

The booty and the captive train
Come in the wake, borne to allay
All nagging doubts this shining day
Where no residual fears restrain.

    The kingdom of the dead
    Has yielded up its dread
    Creators cold of fear.
    The names that chilled the soul,
    The forces of control,
    Are seen as captured here.

    We watch, we hold our breath
    To see the sting of death;
    Hell's very gates of doom!
    And then the empty tomb,
    Grave's victory reversed
    And bonds asunder burst.

    The gaps that we espy
    Who, what is there contained
    Invisibly restrained,
    Too dreadful for the eye?

    The human vassalage
    Of evil follows next;
    Still baffled and perplexed
    At such a final wage.

The sons of war come captive, chained
By power divine disarmed, restrained;
Their banners trail in dust,
Where all rebellion must

End finally.

From ancient times to modern superpowers,
Man's empires have their times, appointed hours;

    The flags they proudly fly
    Sink down to clear the sky.

So Roman eagles, nearby stars and stripes,
The sickled hammer, terrors of all types

    Are utterly

Ground down as total loss;
Sink down before the Cross.

Saint George, in mail, with England's mace
Brings up the rearguard! Dragons' brood
Throughout the centuries subdues
Is yours, our shining knight of grace!

The vision fades. It was sublime;
Within our century and time,
God gently sets us down.
The bishop, shepherd of the flock,
Authority drawn from the rock
Of Simon Peter in succession,
Absolves, and prays in intercession
For all of faith, for Queen and Crown.

Snuffed are the candles; in release
Up from our knees, we part in peace.

But nought can ever be the same
To those of us who stake our claim
In Him, the one and only name
Vouchsafed to us, exceeds all fame.
He has exalted us to be
Co-heirs of all the heavenly,
While still on earth. We leave, restored
In hope and faith in thee, O Lord.

We fear no Usurpator,
O Christ, our Pantocrator!

Easter Sunday, March 30, 1975

---

1. Christ Pantocrator evokes a specific image of Christ in Christian iconography. It is often translated as Christ Almighty, Pantocrator being Greek for "ruler of all."

MORNING

We must look up in faith
To you, O Lord of Grace:
Heal, comfort us; we claim
The power of your name.

This quiet space around
Whose silence is profound
With music shall be filled
That heartache may be stilled.

Bright morning follows night,
And what went wrong comes right;
For sunshine follows rain
And flowers bloom again.

O Living Lord of Light
Go with us through the night
Let joy envelop pain.
There will be song again!

Victor Dirks
For Fran, August 1978

MOURNING

God blesses those that mourn. We are assured
They will be comforted. How deeply glad
Am I there was no break. Let me be sad
Wear public black; this time will be endured.
And where the wound is open, it can mend
In time, by grace and mercy cleansed and dressed.
Not suppurating slowly, not repressed,
It takes its course, the scars will fade and blend.
What is my pain to hers? That suffering
She underwent, how can it fail to bring
Its fruit of faith, the fragile forward thrust
Of sprouting seed arising from the dust?
Tears water it, like gentle showers of rain:
For ashes, beauty, and for loss, a gain.

Victor Dirks
November 1978

Victor's brother Neil

FOR NEIL

Our brother was called home Palm Sunday morn;
To enter into joy, eternal peace.
The Christian hope sustains, is not forlorn,
Provides for restoration and release.

Give him a blessed branch, a palm to bear,
And join the worshipping, acclaiming throng,
Shouting Hosanna, They rejoice, declare
The rider King and Lord, in praise and song.

There is a difference. The palmers are
The ones accepted, and their living Lord
The One who greets; he called them from afar
Brought to his presence, healed, restored.

Thanks be to thee, O Lord; help us perceive
The glory that is given us in thee
A life that is now under your care we grieve
And trusting in your grace, believe.

For Neil, April 2011
VAD

www.ingramcontent.com/pod-product-compliance
Lightning Source LLC
Chambersburg PA
CBHW030908080526
44589CB00010B/204